Ruins of the Heart

Six Longpoems

Ruins of the Heart

Six Longpoems

Kristjana Gunnars

✠ Angelico Press

First published in the USA
by Angelico Press
© Kristjana Gunnars 2022

For information, address:
Angelico Press
169 Monitor St.
Brooklyn, NY 11222
angelicopress.com

ISBN 978-1-62138-843-2 (pbk)
ISBN 978-1-62138-844-9 (cloth)

Cover Design: Michael Schrauzer
Cover Image: Kristjana Gunnars
"the slow passage of sunshine," 2021
acrylic and gold on canvas

CONTENTS

A Moment in Flight

In spring some go to the park and climb the terrace,

but I alone am drifting, not knowing where I am.

Like a newborn babe before it learns to smile,

I am alone, without a place to go.

—Lao Tzu, *Tao Te Ching*

In the garden there is a bower for melancholy,
a hidden garden where I can stay with this sadness.
Wisteria hangs overhead, lilacs emit their scent
and birds wing past at extraordinary speed.

There are fragments of eternity in all passing things.

Saturn is still in the universe with all its moons,
Artemis, goddess of the forest, gives me green
thoughts in a green space.

Tall pines lean slightly in the grey mist of distance,
branches tangle with branches against a backdrop of haze,
water, sky, overhanging rock. I now think

love is a story
that has failure in it, complexity, something
foreign—a story I tell myself
when I am at a loss for words.

When the smooth surface of sentiment cracks,

love itself enters, through
small openings that formed when I broke

down into parts until I no longer
recognized myself. He says
love took you away from your plans—
you lost more than you can bring back.

That is the time you need to be willing
to go under.

What you expect to happen is not what will happen.

If you need to withdraw, he says, you need
to withdraw—love is telling you, with-
draw—

he says *there is gold in the flowing river.*
              Depression distills your nature.

It's exhausting to try to be cheerful when Saturn is near.

If your pain could speak, he asks, what would it say?

The body itself is also poetry: instead of clarity
it gives you depth and music when it speaks—

woundedness is the human condition.
We do not cure disease, he says, *disease
        cures us.*

According to Novalis,
*disease is a musical problem
and requires a musical solution.*

                Liber mundi—
              I have read the same passage over and
              over in this book. Dante himself says

    the wound that Eve opened is the wound that Mary closed.

The complexity of everything is outside:
it strikes unawares: a hurdle of problems
pile into the day, crowding in—

maybe it's the quality of the light
or the sea: small pebbles on the beach,
the sand, the shells and seagrass
and setting sun,
                    the air expanding,
I see the sky, the horizon swells with cloud.

The complexity of everything rushes in like a wave
from the sea, from outside—
its tumult of problems and confusions crashes in.

I know the dead are as much a part of this
community as the living.

> *No one can tell you how to live your life.*
> I'm thinking about what he said.
>
> House of life, house of memory, house
> *made of dawn.*

I'm thinking of the Phoenix: the bird
that rises from the ashes like a blue heron.
I see it
stand still on a rock above the water
waiting for fish, the long, elegant wings

spread out from its body, it lifts itself
into flight, the long neck and beak
stretch forward.

The complexity is human life itself.

      He says *what you have rejected has value:*
            look at it again.

The stone the workers
threw aside suddenly becomes
        the cornerstone,

    the stone that holds up everything.

        The great wings wave
slowly up and down as they begin
to circle over the water:

those wings are wide enough to embrace all
contradictions and paradoxes—

      the heron about to fly is *soulful…*
what is *a soulful being* after all?

I hear the person we choose to be always
comes with its double: *the person we choose*
        not to be.

    The shadow self.

Honour the stories, he says,

    sit
with what is there, not
    what you wish was there.

Much larger worlds are colliding in the cosmos.

Your emotions—fear, jealousy, anger—
are setting limits in your life. Learn them, he says.

Baptism by fire.

There would be too much life to live and too little
depth without them.

Something has gone wrong and needs attention.

Honour the symptoms.

If you lose everything, what is it you have left?

Maybe nothing. Maybe you can drop that salvational fantasy.

Secret wisdom is gone, replaced
with information.

Maybe you can drop that normalcy
        fantasy.

There is scorching heat. The garden has wilted
and dried up. The plants have turned yellow.
The grass does not grow. Parched earth.

I have no desire to try to revive it.
I'm letting it all go—
like the Tao, *heeding the Tao Te Ching*—

there are times it's better to be weak—

life as it was, left unattended,
a garden grown dry and scruffy.

That's how it is after you left.
It's been a peculiar kind of education.

Gain or loss, which causes more pain?
        Lao Tzu is asking.

Those who are attached to things will suffer greatly.

The fir tree towers above low lying clouds,
a long gravel road, a weathered cabin about to fall down—
evergreen branches cradle the fragile roof like the wings of a swan.

You died and I was reborn with a hundred eyes.

        Honouring the departed —
        that was the job to do, the letting go.

There are times it's better to trust the unexpected.

There are times it's better to go ahead and be
who you are not, he tells me.

Perhaps love is like filigree or lace,
intricate, interlocking, many-threaded—
maybe it's like a spider web that catches up everything
        that floats.

Something frightening enough to make us construct
        barricades of moralism.
Fortifications against our fears—

I see the jewelled canopy of night without sleep,
the silken lining of things has a soft feel to it.

I see *when normalcy explodes*
        there is strange meaningfulness—
look at it again, I hear—

voices behind the shutters are whispering
in their own language: your character
cannot change. There is no transformation
of birds in their silver-lined cage.

Your personal philosophy is too neatly wrapped
in silver paper, too tightly tied with burlap twine,
and it leaves no room inside. No room
                                    to breathe.

        The rich brocade of what is called *love*,

has a high pitch to it and also has the dark rumble
of a river flowing under my feet.

There is a glinting light in the firmament
of sleepless nights.
There is a sense of *abduction*.

I go behind a veil, but I can see you at those times.
My thoughts are dark as ruby, distant as turquoise.

        The rewards I find for my vigil are *ordinary*

in the end. The birds sing in their cage—
        abandon the idea of success and understanding.
        That's not what you were meant for, he answers.

What you were meant for—
        wandering, longing, absence, melancholy—

Sometimes when we fall we fall into depths
we never knew existed.

        Mater Dolorosa,
                there are visitors from hell,
and I am drawn into the very thing I least want to experience.

        opus contra naturam—
Sometimes just being yourself is staggering
                in the brilliance of the light you bring.

Change does happen, but not as planned.

I'm told when one form of existence ends it is
felt as an experience of death.

I'm told there is something like a fermentation
that happens in what is called the soul—
when you stop to think things over, *the soul ferments.*

Long ago they said
                    the essence of a person comes from the stars.

If I could project the essence of you onto a whole city
it would be rich and deep, beset
with the scent of coriander and cumin.

I hear *love is a labyrinth*
with a beast alive in its centre—which is also
        an angel.

I have the taste of tarragon in my senses.
I hear the chiming of metal pipes in the wind—

everyday life is about the application of poetics, I hear,
wherein I read my own memory for its poetry.

About applying care to the smallest of things—
a schedule, a breakfast, a pair of shoes.

We cannot thrive in dream, he tells me.
It's only possible to thrive in the everyday
world of concrete earthen things—

we cannot fly.

       We repeat ourselves, our habits, over and over,
     defend ourselves against the onrush of life:
      we follow a deadly pace, our culture,
our culture
     has banished surprise.

Love that was repressed reappears
in objects, in things—a missile, a bomb, a chokehold—

things are not as they appear to be,

innocence is not innocent.

Even though the world continues its every-
day life, it is interrupted by death,
        all forms of death.

Necessary mortifications.

The days begin to resemble a bazaar,

hanging lanterns and brass coffee pots with long handles,
small wooden folding tables, engraved serving trays,
dark rugs to sit on, the smell of wool and nutmeg,
the taste of figs, dates, olives, grape leaves,

coffee boiled in the pot, a sludge of grounds
in a small, decorated glass, loads of sugar. Later

in my room I have time to think my thoughts alone,
the smell of flatbread baking in the café below,
and I'm thinking *the ordinary is the sacred.*

There is a sense of *abandonment,*
    dislocation.

Times when you feel most inferior
                are the important times, I'm told:
                someone else is about to appear
                where your old self was, waning and confused.

All hells are private ones.

If you do not own *unfaithfulness*, he says, it breaks away
from you and is embodied in others.
        Own it, he repeats.

Suddenly the cherry tree that burst into bloom
is lighted as a ball of sun gleams
        through early morning mist. Suddenly

I have time to make concrete decisions
about everyday life.

The sheep of the mind are grazing, wandering—
the latest addiction, the furious dream, the troubling thought—
I know there is an angel that stirs the waters.

I try not to eradicate problems,
the cauldron of moods, impossible relationships, obsessive
                preoccupations—
I try not to take the job of exterminator of the mind.

    Illness itself is a message, remorse
    is a correction, depression is a request
    for necessary change, I hear.

I try not to eradicate the problems.

Submissiveness is not goodness.

Angels are dream figures, their world
is the world of dream, fantasy, imagination—

16

Their wings are spread wide in heaven
according to Dante, and they sing
in unison all the time in *The Paradiso.*

Virtue is not very different
from evil, I'm told. A gun is dangerous mainly
because it fetishizes power: lust
       for power.

The soul is also a gun, he says. Full of potential.

What you don't claim in the end claims you,
     there are no insignificant things in life.

The ghosts of material things
Nerval calls the *objects* displayed in the market:
copper, mother of pearl, amber, coral; antiques,
embroideries, spices. All of it casts a shadow—

I hear it's better to go with the symptoms, listen
to what they say.

We can only work with what is there.

We only know what is true from occasional glances.
A ray of sun that flashes by,
a sudden blast of light that bursts onto the scene
the way a bird might swing past on its way to the nest.

I'm not sure it was a bird after all.
It could have been a mirage. A speck of dust in the eye.

A trick of the brain. A trick that requires we be saved
from being human.

The extraordinary symptoms of being human:
        myths, rituals, poetry of life—

18

Forty days that stretch into fifteen years in the desert,
living an anchorite life with nothing to lean on
but prayer.

Much can be accomplished by not-doing, I hear.

Do not tinkle like jade
or *clatter like stone chimes,* Lao Tzu warns.

Depression is a gift, its thoughts appear only
when it's dark.

Life weathers you naturally, the way wind,
temperature, time weather a barn

and youthful enthusiasm becomes a burden you need
relief from, relief from
                    the unbearable lightness of being.

The lightness of the hazy forest and the rain
of dark words sailing down in rows from the sky.

No, you do not always have to be cheerful, he says.
Remember, it's an effective form of repression
to give a thing excessive honour.

Good people do not know they are good.

I wanted to be swept away
into that other world where eagles fly overhead,
where rain falls on leaves, where clouds
become wispy and disappear.

I'm told when a person is focussed only on himself
it's because he does not love himself—
he is an empty vessel where all things have poured out
into the rain.

Into the falling rain of words from a dark sky
onto the sand where waves wash in
blindly, effortlessly—

There are already enough names, Lao Tzu says,
we need to know when to stop—

I'm told love is an event, love makes the ground fertile
with memories, with images; makes us

able to fly.

20

My own wings were far too weak for that, Dante says
when he tries to look into the light at the very end
of *The Paradiso.*

He says love cures us of a life emptied of others—

when love arrives we are unsettled and disturbed,
we are on the tragic side of life at last,
our plans are shaken and sad, and still,

*the ultimate cure for being alive
        comes from love,* he says.

Fraser and Salmon

In 1977, Jorge Luis Borges gave seven lectures on seven nights. The book of these lectures is titled *Seven Nights*, where he mimics the idea of *The Thousand and One Nights* in Arabic literature, and has drawn much material from Arabic sources as well as Buddhist sources. I have read this book many times and have quoted from it before, but here I have used it as a thread to tie the parts of this long poem together. I have quoted occasionally from the first five lectures, and left the salient idea of the last two for the "postscript" at the end.

This long poem started off as a series of poems ostensibly concerned with relationships and romantic love. However, the manuscript evolved into a series of tied poems that make up one longpoem in two threads. These are imagerially presented as two rivers, which are actual rivers in the B.C. Delta; the Fraser River and the Salmon River that criss cross at the town of Fort Langley. There is a Buddhist Temple here too, which is the famous International Buddhist Temple in Richmond, B.C.

Along with the thoughts of Borges, I have made use of some poetic ideas I found in books on Sufi wisdom. All these "borrowed" notions, sometimes rephrased by me, are italicized. Sufi thinking is much concerned with the idea of love and its transformations, and the idea of the illusory nature the Self and reality. Those were articulations of goals I was trying to reach in the first place with the original poems, so referring to them allowed me to underline what I was trying to make happen in the poem.

The first of Borges' set of lectures is on Dante's *Commedia*. One or two of his thoughts on that major literary work have found their way into the present poem. But what Borges says of *The Divine Comedy* is worth repeating, and not for any special reason, but just because of the view it presents of reading in general: "The *Commedia* is a book that everyone ought to read. Not to do so is to deprive oneself of the greatest gift that literature can give us; it is to submit to a strange asceticism. Why should we deny ourselves the joy of reading the *Commedia*?"

24

Light has filled the ruins of this heart.
Let this universe of mine be shattered.

—Jalāl ad-Dīn Rūmī

****

No one told me it would be like this.

No one told me the sun would shine relentlessly
and the river would be so still
                              and the island—

the island would be called *Bride's Island*.

There's a lot you don't know when the day begins
that you are wise to by evening.

There are nine clouds in the sky.

> On the first night he says: *we are made
> for art, we are made for poetry.*

Just because they are predicting the earth's demise
as if it were a rare species no one cares about,

or just because they are creating atmospheric models
of *nuclear winter* based on forest fires,

doesn't mean we have nowhere to go.
Does it?

> *because the subject of poetry is friendship.*

When our love ends—because it is love,
I know it is from all the signs in the sky—
when our love ends will it be ours alone?

A secret held by only you and me, to

       leave the house of those who talk too much
       and go to the one where people are silent...

****

Take the fruits that are in the words,
they have the scent of musk.

We went walking in a small town that really
looked like a small town. A picture image
of itself. Little shops made of wood and painted
signs and cafés with park benches, some
out in the street, all over the sidewalk.

He said he was a sad figure, *forever condemned*
to that town filled with the absence of a friend.

It was just a cliché small
town but for some reason
it was also

a place where huge ideas
are anchored. They no longer run the ferry
to Bride's Island, back and forth.

There has been a lot of movement of peoples
over time, from river to river, island to island.
We are not the first. Everything has become ordinary.

Except the secrets we hold in our hearts.

The long day that ferries us and the long night

that lets us go until we are nowhere and have lost
all knowledge and all sense of direction.

We wander from golden ear to golden ear
in some dream of the past and future meeting here.

War has come and gone and come and gone
in succession, always the same war.
I no longer count the ways a person can die—

I understand *in Hell nothing can be beautiful.*

I only count the ways you
can abandon you,

—become like melting snow
wash yourself of yourself.

With love your inner voice will find a tongue
growing like a silent white lily in the heart…

****

At times you have to close your eyes to the glare
of desire, it shines like metal
that catches the sun on its passing.

> On the second night he wonders *how astonishing it is*
> *that we wake up each morning,*
> *that we wake up each morning sane.*

I whisper my dreams to the cottonwood tree
so they can fly away with the breeze rustling the leaves
and be heard above the clouds.

Up there only the precious ears are listening.
What I am craving is floating far away

where the wind shifts patterns, changes direction,
surprises, refuses and fulfills all at once.

> At night in dream, each one of us receives
> *a little personal eternity.*

We were out in the street among the town people
walking around being clichés of themselves.
They were selling stalactites

from caves in Peru, creepy brown stones
that looked like eyeballs. They were sweeping
the courtyard with straw brooms.

Victor Hugo also talked about *le cheval noir de la nuit*—
the black horse of night.

The sun was shining. They were closing shop.

He said you do not have to be asleep in a nightmare;
our waking life abounds
in terrible moments—

Remember me and I will remember you.

****

Every night I see the space station passing by.
The lights are blinking and it has great speed.

You were asking if time stops above the clouds
in space. We were wondering if time is real.

I remember saying the astronauts come back younger.

On the third night he says
even numbers are evil omens—

I know you can live your life in both directions.
I learned that when I saw the Fraser and the Salmon

trying so hard to touch below our feet.

All of this is about love.

Desire written in strokes of a brush, marks
of a pen, gunshots of a printing press
firing in all directions.

Rose and mirror and sun and moon—where are they?

He remembered to say the Romantic movement begins
when someone in Normandy or someone in Paris
reads *The Thousand and One Nights*.

****

It was Rumi who said: *Polish your heart*
for a day or two; make that mirror
your book of contemplation.

The cottonwood tree stood its ground in the wetland,
water pooling at its feet, grasses and leaves floating

in small waterways along the field. The cottonwood stood
and waited for us at the bend, I saw it waiting, arms out-

stretched, head shaking, *what took you so long?*
Why did we take so long to die like this

and be born like this and float away
like the dandelion fluff wafting by?

On the fourth night he quotes James Joyce
who said *History is a nightmare*
from which I am trying to awake.

He also says Siddhartha at age thirty *woke up*
and became a Buddha.

I am left in the dry heat of summer,
in the searing sunshine, burning.

* * *

It was the year the Amazon forest burned
to the ground, thousands, hundreds of thousands
of fires blackened the skies to the south.

I didn't know what to say then. I was truly
silenced, the way the songbirds are and I have not
seen or heard a songbird all summer long.

> *The Buddha said we must pull the arrow out.*
> He asked what is the arrow? The arrow is the universe.

> The arrow is the I
> *of everything to which we are chained.*

I heard you sing in the kitchen, you were cutting
avocado slices on the wooden board, you sang
and I had never heard that voice before,
the strong, clear tones that fell like velvet
on the waning afternoon. The light was going out,

the darkness was descending in the courtyard
with the grass and trees, on the street with street
lamps in a row, cars parked at the curb clear
to the end, all the way to the railroad tracks.

Just for a split moment I heard
the decades of silence come crawling out
the way creatures crawl out of a tree trunk when it burns.

I heard the decades of silence when I did not sing
and you did not sing, decades lost, songs unsung.

A silence that has flown towards me from the leaves of trees,
of cottonwoods on the banks of the Fraser,
and spread its wings as it washed the air
with flower petals, pink and maroon, sailing.

> I am told by Schopenhauer the world is a dream.
> *We must stop dreaming it.*

We were like two monks in the clearing, alone
and deprived, without the song of the birds
and without the trees in the jungle,

without the world we failed to hold.

> *A hundred important affairs have shattered you,*
> *thousands of desires and concerns are spread everywhere—*
>
> *you must unite the scattered parts by means of love...*

****

You wanted to die
when I encountered you on the banks of the Fraser.

You envisioned yourself closing your eyes,
dropping your head gently and fading off—

It was a long-standing thought, it was a plan you had
when I walked over across the dry grasses and scrub brush.

And after such a long time of emptied eyes
you woke, you came back

from the edge of the dark green river
and the labyrinth of hemlocks, cedars, Douglas fir,

the forests we got lost in, oblivious to time and direction.
We did not want to be found. We wanted to be lost.

      I said if I were a Buddhist monk I would be thinking
      at this very moment that *I had just begun to live*....

We took in all the seasons in one day
and we drank sunlight like the flowers do

that open their mouths to the light.
We encountered the ouroboros, the snake biting
its tail in the grass, the bear
and the eagle and the whale sailed in circles around us.

Waves rose in the sea below us
and crashed onto the rocky shore. We watched the glow

of evening as if it had nothing to do with us.
The warmth of the air enfolded us like a careful guardian.

Amazing as it sounds, the songbirds, the rushing sea,
the hissing snake, struck the air like thunder.

> *Another night is passing away,*
> *another day is rising—*
>
> *tell me I have spent the night well—*
> *and if not, so I can mourn what is lost.*

He then compares the state of Nirvana to an island
surrounded by torments.

****

When you left I noticed the black velvet
sky above us, the deep darkness of night
in the hemispheres, without stars, without
moon, depleted space empty of light.

     On the fifth night he says there are as many Bibles
     as there are readers. The text, he says,
          is the changing river of Heraclitus.

I was distracted by the velvet night, almost
forgot to say good bye as you got in
the car and waved. I was looking up then

     at the thought attributed to Nietzsche
     that the moon is a monk
     who gazes enviously at the earth—

and remembered we were talking about empti-

ness at the Buddhist Temple, where we sat
in the gardens among bonsai trees and
pines. Green grass stretched before us
and tall plum trees along the perimeter

facing the small farm where monks
grow apples and strawberries and blue-
berries. The baskets in front of the deities
were emptied of offerings earlier

in the day, the flowers depleted, some
placed before Avalokiteśvara or the Great
Buddha in the big hall. It was the end
of the day, they were about to close

the Temple grounds. When I looked up
a lone monk in grey robes walked
across the courtyard with determination
in front of the latticed windows of the dining

room hall. You told me at the Zen
retreat in Hawaii you lost weight
and never got it back. Your body decided
on emptiness. Your eyes were sorrow-

ful too, your hands and shoulders
tired by now. It's been a long life
filled with attempts to grasp at nothing-
ness and its meaning—

A life of walking on rugs of stars.

Light has filled the ruins of this heart,
let this universe of mine be shattered—

****

In the temple garden twisted oaks
give shade to lonely worshippers of love

that sit like deities inside the pagoda, lips
menacingly red, eyebrows furrowed with fear.

The bamboo groves, small and scattered
along the incline of grass and sun, pro-

voke the afternoon sky, so blue, so deep
and bright. Concrete benches line up

where worshippers sit down and wait
as if for execution, so dark in thought, so

deeply in love. The walking path strewn
with small bushes and weeds welcomes us

in its own twisted way. The green of late summer
goes on to the horizon, the alders and firs,

now careless with the end of things,
feel the onrush of unsettling winds—

in the time of eastern hurricanes and northern
tornadoes and talk of looming catastrophe

can love survive such times, can love
endure an apocalypse?
Empty questions, as I look at your face, now sad

with the thought of a lifetime of mistakes,
you said, a lifetime of mistakes.

      The Phoenician sailor said: judge me as a man
      whom the ocean has broken.

When my pen attempts to describe this state,
the pen is shattered and the paper torn to shreds.

——Jalāl ad-Dīn Rūmī

Postscript

On the sixth and seventh nights Borges himself says
the ancient food of poets is

humiliation, unhappiness, discord, those things
were given to them to transform,

but particularly unhappiness. Happiness itself
does not need to be written.

Happiness exists on its own.

****

Everything perishes . . . not that everything perishes at some particular moment, but rather it is forever perishing, since it cannot be conceived except as perishing.

—Abū Hjāmid al-Ghazālī

Threadbare

I walk in the fields now, fields
the color of lime and neon in the sun
as if lit from within, fields of spring.

I can smell the flying dust and straw
in the heat of midday when there is no rain
and the horizon extends to the end of my vision—

everything that moves: clouds, water,
leaves, moon, stars, animals and also the wind—
everything that moves is alive.

Is the sky father or mother? Is the water
lily really a star that fell from heaven, is
the milky way really snow that flies

off a bear's coat as it crosses the bridge
      of dead souls?

Stones hewn from a quarry nearby,
sand pulled from the hillside there, blankets
made of the wool of llamas in the pastures—

these are the only things I had—
and the leaves, nuts and berries in the garden.

I did not have anything else.

Perhaps a black bowl of water, marigold
blossoms floating there, only this.

I wanted to be free in a world where no two
things are the same. No snowflake
is like any other. No two hands are the same.
No two pieces of wood have the same grain.

Threadbare.
I lay claim to nothing.

Someone *vanishes* in all this, one of us,
as if it were a burning, this becoming, this existence,

another's otherness: you see it suddenly, slowly,
and yet that other bursts into view
the way sunlight does

from night into day, and *vice versa*.

The deep black of ebony, the yellow of pine,
red of cherry, white of silvery ash:

Wood.

It's in the green fields I think of endless
loops I've outlived, when I see
rows of poplars along the drive
and lines of grape vines below the meadow.

I can smell them grow: I swear I can hear them,
buds bursting to make room for new, fresh leaves-
I can hear the starlings swish across the sky in formations.

We are bereaved with compulsion,
a cliff-side where we crash ourselves into fragments.

Or I do, and I can tell you of my failures all night long,

there are so many, we could talk until morning.

Sometimes life absorbs light and does not
reflect.

Walnut, chestnut, maple—
wood.

The days grow warmer all the time, the world
lights up with its own demise
all around us.

Nothing here is *reasonable*,

it wasn't supposed to be. No one goes looking for
a wound.

Peppermint, willow, conifer,

a flower-filled pasture.

Linen, jute, wild rosemary.

I know I've longed for this landscape the way
a child longs for its lost mother or a soul
waits for a promise not kept to come true.

These fields go on
effortlessly before me like a dream.

I have to look at them many times now, the green
of growing grasses and the pink of early dusk.

Watery realms of peppermint, dew-
covered spring grass.
Every moment that passes is *irretrievable.*
You can't get it back when it's gone.
For that reason I have a sense of sorrow all the time,
a feeling something has been abolished,

some life spark has been put out
or some species has gone extinct.

Every moment is like that
when a disappearance has occurred.

A bluebell-carpeted forest,
cotton and linen.

Parchment. Cold tea.
Day and night.

Stones and dried branches.

I try to begin again. Pretend what happened
never happened and now is the first time, once
again.

Every embrace is an embrace of something

going away into the dark. I reach and yet
what I try to touch doesn't yet exist.

I know nothing is there and I also know something is,

something I can't touch, however
far I extend my hands, arms, fingers: a black wind

rushes through the jagged cliffs and makes a high-
pitched sound like a voice of the earth singing
some tune never heard before, a song of sirens,

a wind that rushes across oceans of green
and tangled branches of trees
like a mad compulsion sighing.

Hessian and sawdust. Bark chips.
There is a difference between the smoothness
of silk and the roughness of raw
linen.

Texture, touch, is all I know.

In the end I leave the grounds behind
as if I were a watchman now done for the day,
and head back into the night where no answers arrive

except the memory of green, answers once true.
Time in these fields is endless,
nothing ever ends. I step through clouds

of dry sand, small stones feel jagged under my feet
and a purple haze is in the spring air.

A hand-thrown life,
earthen,

engulfed by what seems like a dis-ease
but no one is sick. I'm better than well,
more alive than alive and I
know it.

This is a wellness I can hardly bear. Maybe
it was better when I was just living,
before in time, when I was not *more* than living,

when a routine was just a routine and a dream
just a dream that meant nothing and an event was just

one of those things you do to wile away the days
and nights. Especially the nights.

The skeleton of everything.

Geraniums, rosemary, St John's Wort,
dried lavender and orange.

Now I'm forced to look darkness in the eye.

I'm learning the art of dying. So slowly, more slowly than the sun,

more slowly than the moon and the north star and the fir trees
dancing in the fog of distance where no one can breathe.

I have a feeling now living and dying are the same: there's no
difference. Life drives itself forward like a harsh windstorm

and crashes itself into pieces on the black cliffs.

Cinnamon bark.
A dish of damp stones. Wild grasses.

I think I could stand under the wisteria blooms forever.
I could smell their perfume and observe their graceful foldings.

The small bushes in the dark shadows, I could watch them too,

all of it, stones, grasses, leaves, blossoms, all of it.

I could stand here and think as if all of time were mine-
I want to think about eternity, so dry and soft.

I wander in my own landscape as if it were a dream.
I didn't mean to be here. It was never meant to be.

It's such a strange experience to outlive time like this,

so strange.

Black Rose With Rain

There is a shadow in the world.

The darkness is cold, *and our thoughts ripen*
            like fruit on a tree of stars.

A bare lightbulb hangs from a cord
above a scuffed canteen table from nowhere
on a flagstone floor—ordinary
irregularity. Life in small details.

All stable, unchanging, without surprise.
I find myself in *a world of autonomous speakers.*

Nothing takes me by surprise any more,
not even death will do that.
Death will come at the right time
whenever it is there: any time,

there is no such thing as non-time any more
or the wrong time.
There is no wrong time for anything.
No wrong place for anything. Galvanized

metal, old French monastery benches,
canvas panels for walls.
Small spaces, small moments.

The duration of things is vast
but never empty. There is no such thing
as empty duration.

At the turn of the century, French shepherds
kept the sun away with linen umbrellas
of unevenly dyed indigo. When closed,
the deep folds of fabric amass a dark blue shade.

I'm thinking *a woman cannot be loyal to civilization,*
after all.

I know we are going nowhere
no matter how fast we move—
there is no conclusion. We lost the art
of *concluding.*

There are no completions, no thresholds,
we undergo no transitions,
we are beyond those barriers.

> *Nature is silent; the voices of nature are*
> *dumb,* and you ignore her intent
>   at your own expense.

The old chair is torn, the burlap slit
and horsehair escapes where stitches
unfurl. Imperfection is a virtue, they say,
things worn, torn, faded. I rest quietly

in this old space, arms extended, eyes
to the sky where the white window opens
to the haze of day. Time can work blindly
on earthly things. Have you noticed

there was a regime change not so
recently, say a hundred years ago, roughly,
we went from God to human—

or everyone else did, rather,
because we, somehow, you and I
are standing in a lasting present.

Did you notice things are still around us?
Just around us. Everywhere else
time flies. Time rushes somewhere, where
I don't know. Time whizzes around

except around us, where time rests
like a picture,
black rose with rain.

> *Let us hear the discourse of the meaningless—*
> *the silenced:*

you cannot exploit a nature that speaks to you.

It's the story that matters.

They say there is an emptiness to avoid,
a yawning nothing,
but we are not there, there is nothing
we need to avoid, you and I.

What I would like is to linger a while
in quiet contemplation.

Who is designing this pattern, and who
is handing out copies
    one after another, over and over

       in the silence of nature?

One by one the others leave the earth,
they float upwards, away from Terra.

I don't know why they are floating off.

Perhaps meaning itself has lost gravity
the way we lose ozone and ice and wetlands,
not even slowly any more.

Have you noticed the weightlessness of things?

Did you know the magnetic field moved away?

Everything has lost importance
when you can't decide what's important
any more, it's gone
and then there is nothing to complete—

no direction is more meaningful than any other.

Impermanence has become permanent.
There lurks a latent totalitarianism in reason.

Like the soft linen, crumpled and shaded
on the bed and pillows embroidered by someone
wild and lonely in a cottage nearby. Five cows
line up facing the window.

It used to be God who made things happen
and go in a certain direction.

Now things are just whizzing around.

Did you notice how you thought time was going faster?

But it is not. Time is not moving,
it's just how you feel. *Rushed.*

S V Laurent 8
the grain sack says, home textiles
with intrigue. Oak and barley,
Japanese kaya mosquito net
of hemp covers the window,

keeps the glare of midday out.

Nothing lasts. Everything lasts, simultaneously.

Linger a while with me.

Let us not think of other things—

let us only think of the scent of the rose
and the cool touch of raindrops
we hear falling beyond the curtain
onto the rustling leaves.

In the mustard yellow sunlight of yesterday
and people on balconies,
one lighted window,
> *just like a songbird that stands still*
> *and quiet in a ray of sunshine.*

I wanted to warn them as they floated
away from earth: if you live so fast
you die fast.

The faster you go the faster you get nowhere—

rescue reason from its success.

The self-interest of it. The political power of it.

They think they are going to an event
that has to be experienced—
jute sacking covers the seat
where indigo cushions from Ghana lie
bedridden in star-like constellations,

but it's not the event itself they go to—
it's the time before,

the time that is not the event—

that is the precious time.
Against the night sky, glorious
deep blue. Beautifully uneven.

If many events follow each other closely
time becomes fragmented
and there is no time to linger.

There are these two powerful technologies:
literacy and Christian
exegesis.

They took nature into their mouths and swallowed—
space monsters.

Linger a while with me,
let us not think of other things
if we can, think only of you and me

and this quiet moment: the sound
of flowing water: the scent of lilac
everywhere, our patchwork existence.
Fog rolls in this time of day,
day stitched to night with thread of mist and cloud.

Pieces of linen scraps hang where
the white light shines through.

Gingham and lace, purple checked.

There is an untold story waiting,
    the other story.

The medicine bundle story,
where missions fail and people
don't understand.

Let us walk along the path
strewn with autumn leaves
among the rooted trees that line the avenue.

Let us experience leisure,
let us feel the heavy arms of existence
lighten.

Let us be *walkers*:
it's not the place we go to but the path we take,

not the destination but the prayer,
not the place but the penance

where meaning is.
A typhoon just passed through the city
where paths are thoroughfares,
where aftermath is another word for
calm.

The snow tasted like stars and moons
and smelled like pine needles—
tasted like empty city streets
and always a mother at a window, calling,

and behind the *littera* is *moralis*, and behind
moralis is the *anagogue:*

her personal exegesis in a time of human speech.

White linen curtains are hung with jute string
on a metal pole to alter
the mood, and the walls of our circumference
are off-white. I am told everything

ʒaps through the world now
because all things rush into the present moment
until there is no present.

There is no harmonious mix of anything.
Lithuanian kitchen cloths, Tokyo linens,
raspberry pink, mushroom grey
when held up to the light like that.

They grew flax and made linen in
Lithuania since the middle ages, I know,
it's a prestigious heritage.

They just said God is speaking to you
through nature. Nature itself
does not speak, they said. You are alone
here on Terra and leaves and trees and roses
are your book—

Everything has a different colour,
a different scent and timbre

now that we are in this crystalline moment
where everything is beautiful
and beauty is owed nothing.

Beauty only comes forward in lingering,
in quiet solitude, slowly,
far away from thoroughfares,
away from noise.

Let us stay a while,
let us not think of other things.

The light is waiting behind a tree.

The light is hiding in the shadow of spring.

I don't think human beings are superior any more,
she calls out.

Give us a new language. Let us learn it.
The language of birds.

The light captures all the varied shades
in their obvious decay
when reflected in the mirror of our blindness.

From this house,
the bitter slave of time, with the night
of a thousand years in his tired eyes
walks out.

I am told even time can decay,
I am told time itself has a blind spot.

Let us walk in the blind spot, you and I.

Many things, most things get better
with age.

The celestial links in the chain may have come
undone, she said.

Do you see the angel on the way?
How it hovers darkly,
how it makes no predictions.

I think the angel is there *to tear us from death*
the way linen tears and burlap is torn
from the greedy hands of the new.

The angel has been evacuated from the stars,

it's telling us to be *sensual—*

be sensual.

    Evolution has no goal.

This is the dwelling place, this lengthening moment.

Time will stop.

The tin trunk stands at the foot of the bed,
pale blue, rust red.

We are on the outermost fringes.

I don't know why they are yawning.
I don't know why they find indifference
in all things, yawning indifference.

Since time has lost its anchor
and is pulled into the currents so fast
they are rushing away without aim.

Let us be walkers
and walk the path,
the country road that has no destination.

Striped buffing disks lie unused in the workshop,
boxes are stacked with books.

Let us pluck that flower, say the houses
to the night,
        the flower of the moon.

        All the knowledge they produced created
        the silence of trees and the soliloquy
                of man.

Let us be going nowhere
just now, let us not think of other things
but books and poetry, old stanzas,
faded print.

Quietly we can follow the path of the sun,
we can take the course of the pale moon,
we can rest under the silken stars
ravaged by age in their distance,

where beauty is owed nothing.
Beauty just is.

I am told all that is meaningful hides—
truth and beauty will only appear
when no one is searching.

Only in contemplation,
that is what I hear, the sound,
the sonorous truth,
the scent of beauty,

the sensuous instant prolonging itself
indefinitely.
A burgundy canopy covers the French
four-poster, the bag we travelled with
crumples folded on the ottoman.

Let us be like the trees,
slow and constant,
let us stay

and stretch our limbs to the sky
where the angel hovers darkly
to *wrest us from death.*

The patisserie stand is out of place here,
an old oil painting hardly keeps up with time,
its roses almost invisible.

I don't know why the others are drifting away.
I don't know why they have let go.
The anchor is untied, I don't know why

they are tearing themselves away
so fast, they rush headlong

away from earth, one after another.

Perhaps they were afraid of pain,
Homo Doloris, it was not for them.

I think it's true: the noise of rushing away
has made them hard of hearing.

So you and I, let us be like the trees,
let us stay and stretch our limbs.

The snow does not remember—

Leave the storage boxes closed, those
full of bills and papers, let the hat-box alone
and the bonnets and portraits of lost time,
for beauty is owed nothing.

Let us go down the country path,
let us not think of other things.

I am told only *leisure* will make us human.
Only in fragrant stillness
will we hear the sound of the birds

in a world of irrational silence.

When the others go adrift like that
they are only able to hear what is direct,

language will become *a scream*—
the only thing they hear now is the scream.

It was not for them
to linger in loving attentiveness.

The dried flowers have lost their life.

So let us be still,
like a picture, a portrait of a brunette
who looks at us like she would look out
the window at the fog

and in it, see

a black rose with rain.

She says the great room of her thoughts
is filled with snow, and the words
*   are falling into a well*
*   of loneliness.*

Let us reach out our limbs
in loving attentiveness
in the deep scent of the rose,
in the cool touch of raindrops—

let us be like the trees, let us learn

a new language, tell

a new story.

Under a Winter Sky

PREFACE

The Sufi poet Hafiz tells the story of two bears having a conversation in the forest. One bear says to the other, with a note of envy in his voice, have you heard about R? R has become famous. He dances and performs in a golden cage for millions of people. The other bear thought about it for a while and then began to weep.

The microtexts in this collection began as poems but evolved into their present form over the winter months one year. There is a story embedded throughout, a narrative, but mostly these are meditations that have happened during daily walks in the lower mainland of B.C. While walking, the mind is free to roam and memory plays its tunes and images without hindrance. I have enjoyed various books of poems by others that have been framed as meditations while walking, and in the past I have engaged in a study of "walking poetry" such as that of Basho and the haibun tradition.

When a manuscript takes a long time to develop, much of what you read and converse about ends up finding its way into your writing. I am somewhat indebted to thoughts on walking by Henry David Thoreau, but I have also leaned on some of the ideas expressed by Walter Benjamin in his *Arcades Project* about the metropolis and the flâneur. I have had the poems of Hafiz to lean on as well, constant companions during this writing. A series of discussions and readings on the ideas of American schematic and transcendental theorists also worked their way into these texts. Several friends have generously contributed thoughts and enthusiasm over the months for specific ideas treated here as well.

The story of the two bears that opens this preface has several levels at which it is to be understood. The basic idea is that what human beings live and work for, the worldly rewards they seek, are actually things that will imprison them. Happiness is not happiness; success is not success; glory is not glory, and so forth. What a person should strive for is almost invisible: it is an invasion of the self and the body by a transcendent spirit which cannot be seen but can be felt. Ultimately, the only thing worth striving for in the mind of Hafiz is love. A sensibility that can be discovered when you remove yourself from the crowds and seek solitude walking on a path under a wintry sky.

1

what the trees are whispering

I walk a path that seems to lead to distant beaches *where thought becomes my beautiful lover.* The path beckons forward, ringed by winter trees and small puddles down the middle. Time moves so slow I can't see the dust settling. I see it only after it's there, layers of star debris. I know it's almost too late for everything. The world seems like a superficial place—a place of *wish images*—until you wake up from your sleep. You see things can move in all directions at once, there are no directions. Solid buildings in the distance serve transitory purposes. What is novel is that things replicate themselves—not just thoughts and feelings but living things. They return to the beginning again and again. It's almost too late for new beginnings, and yet. They are busy *bringing the countryside into town.* You and I, we have been away from each other all our lives. We have never met and we met a long time ago, distant eras ago. That's how it seems. There is a *phantasmagoria* we can enter and be distracted, but only temporarily. Nothing is for sure, except that the breeze is strengthening in the black hours of early dawn, the branches thin and frail against the moon-lit sky. The hermit in me is walking. They say *every walk is a kind of crusade.*

2

ten thousand steps

Every walk you take, I am told, should be thought of as your last. *To walk as if you will never return.* I went out that way into the wintry air. There wasn't much I could do about the rain pouring down, the soaked-up shoes and wet hair, I just let it happen, the wind and water. I was enjoying this alienation from myself like someone who knows *the ten thousand positions of divine love.* A cold gust from an open window lay still in my memory of us munching on french fries and broccoli soup, you with your pale ale, the day forming in its dark grey guise. I hardly know what to say about anything, about the stars or sun, about the way I feel after all these years—a little numb from the hard-hitting elements. Some things are not easy to face when you get down to it, yet so *fashionable.* But fashion, you say, is there *to defend the rights of the corpse.* What they call the *sex appeal* of the inorganic. It gets easier the more I learn about daily life, those not special things, finally no longer inside an illusion. The way I'm learning to think of you too, that part of daily life that cycles through the day on rainy streets, water splash-ing from puddles and trucks drenching us with mud as they roar past, traffic congested all down Johnston Avenue, bumper to bumper. Even traffic has a philosophy. I know when all is flooded, love is a life raft. But I walk like this, silently. They say you need a *dispensation from heaven* to be a walker. A special allotment. To walk. To remember *not to die again.*

3

the sky is no place to lose your wings

As with *the scent of a lover's body*, sometimes I walk out but my spirit stays back. The fresh air full of cold droplets does nothing to revive me or bring my mind along. I wanted to put you out of my memory, to avoid you, to forget yesterday, but I'm told that forgetting will never happen. I don't understand this mirror world and how often a thing is reflected in reflection, how frequently a mirror image mirrors itself. It seems normal to think there is an inside and an outside and these are different, that we saunter in and out all the time, but when a *flâneur* stands on the threshold she is *both* inside and outside. What is *out there* is also *in here*, everything mirrored in me and in you. Hold onto this book: *it contains wonderful secrets.* We can never be separate, we can never part, you and I, even though I have wanted to avoid this thought, this narcotic of time, this looming eye contact with you. I have a vague understanding there are angels of a sort always going back and forth, busy in the wayside brush, but I don't see them, too busy thinking of more solid things, and the world flows by me *like the smoke of a cigar.*

4

adages for a snowy day

They say go like the old prophets went, into nature, with your sacks of old shoes and cucumbers. I see the rain as if from afar and then a slight dusting of snow. Little pearls live in the shells of words. The sky is white, the tall trees ponder. At first everything is just curiosity, finding a voice in what others overlook, finding energy in the way past and present interact. Being *a lover to the unreal*. When I look at a thing I look at myself, I give expression to myself. If I remove a thing from its context, is it still the same thing? If I put an object somewhere else, is it still the same object? Everything hovers in mid-air, everyone here is a guest *lost in heaven*. A slight wind disturbs the thin branches swaying without rhythm. My balance is thrown off. We are always in a state of culture shock. Trial and error is the best teacher. We communicate by hidden codes. I try to reach to the heart of this thought—it's such a long reach. The table is set but no one arrives. Error is an old friend. We have come to terms with each other, uneasy terms. I am living in the residue of a snowed-in dream world. The snow continues to fall hour after hour. The tall trees are floating. I am told nature has a magnetism—that when it leads you, you go the right way.

5

the million candles

Every sunset which I witness inspires me with the desire to go to a West as distant and as fair as that into which the sun goes down.
—Henry David Thoreau

He says the sun is a Western pioneer. I want to follow. But when I do, I go down into the horizon and never come back. That is the way love dies. When love dies my attitude becomes pure reaction. Escapism appeals to me. Eclectic seems like a good word. I want to remove everything, leave only a few items—a wooden Buddha cross-legged on the window sill, an Egyptian pumice stone. His imprint is in all the rooms he inhabited. He etched every moment of my existence *before I knew it myself*. I am unable to sort out the separate stories, they blur and fuse together. His departure seems like *an act of terrorism*. What do I want among my fingers now? *You want to secure the city against civil war*. The dead will exploit the living *like a factory owner exploits the means of production*. If my surroundings were now a temple, I hear myself say, if all the gods now answered, lingered a while on earth— the earth that is characterized by unrest—then all of my love's objects would *demand to be worshipped*. But only silence answers. Only a wind-blown airiness can be heard. The wind is whirling to the player's flute and dust circles fast *like illumined planets*.

6

the appearance of distance

I watched the moon this morning, before dawn, curl its way across the western horizon, its early arc, a large red lantern lit for the night soon to go out. Moon on fire. I saw how it went behind the tall pines, glinting now and then between branches. The rice was on. Miso soup was cooling in its cup. The neighbour's pale white light spilled onto the blackberries and the night flight trainees were circling their last rounds before landing, blinking their feeble lights above us. I watched with the alienation of *the future inhabitants of the metropolis*. I wondered what the blood moon looked like from up there, in full view. It's all about perspective, or where you are when you see things, or what the moon says to you if you're high or low in the sky. Did I see things right? Did I hear what I heard? I wondered what is their final destination *if not Death*? Is their destination not *the New*? All I needed was one moment to know things are further away than you think. What the moon told me today before it went out like a light behind the thick pillars of trees and into the hard earth, where everything ends up buried in ash. I remembered being told that thoughts are as ethereal as the sky, and *love is like an inland sea*.

> *There is nothing in your mind you have not invited in.*
> —Hafiz (Shams-ud-din Muhammad)

7

dancing white birds

When the swallows come back to Capistrano I stand in the light of the full moon and watch the first two morning stars, *as if in religious intoxication*. What will become of them in the long run? There is a long run for everything. When you said good bye, that's the day the swallows flew out to sea. I have not seen them all winter, *as if winter never existed*, though I have looked. I walk along the water where the sun sets and the moon rises, the lonely beach where I spend my days and my black nights in the light of the moon. The abandoned doorways of old houses, every door a *door of romance*, seem to wait for a new spring. Watching for the dark small forms of cliff swallows at the Mission San Juan Capistrano, where I step on the whispering gravel paths around the stone and stucco and brick walls, mud nests, wild roses and water lilies in the pond; Saint Junipero Serra and the wall of bells ringing in the spring, this *ideal image of elegance*, this *grim sadistic touch*, my attention spirited away *as if by violence*. Once again it is the season that comes after the long winter months, when you said good bye and the swallows flew out to sea in their *superior beauty*. What will become of them in the long run? What I thought was rain is not rain: it is *a thousand swaying arms*.

8

something of me is falling like stars

At night when I look to the north-western sky the horizon is bathed in a dim white glow. Lights of the city spread and drift into space where they go forward endlessly. The city pulses in the dark at a mysterious distance as if *bathing in the sea*. The first planes and air tankers glide in and out, solemn and cumbersome, as early morning begins. Their blinking lights circle above the airport in the western horizon in no *compromise with hurry*. Nothing else moves, reminding me there is a larger world beyond the glow of the city, filled with different scents and textures, where the air is thicker than the air I breathe here, where the light is redder, where the temperature rises into extremes. A world that is large, larger still than the moon that hovers even beyond dawn, the moon that won't let go when day comes in its tyranny and all the city lights have melted into the blazing heat of fires that burn up the horizon, vibrating *as fully as possible*. Wild. *Another name for the West.* The air is failing us. We suffocate, even as *the most alive is the wildest* and in the darkness that is filled with a million candles *the angels know you well*.

9

when the sun became a jewel

As I walk in the wetlands where songbirds and waterfowl go down-river two by two I understand *we enter a swamp as a sacred place.* I remember we met by chance, but what was our chance meeting one Saturday morning while the leaves were still on the trees and white-capped waves on the sparkling sea were dancing? As I walk I wonder, is there an alternative to chance itself: the feeling that we are thrown in a direction by some force we didn't understand in the first place, and still don't know what it is to be *thrown.* Where is this invisible hand? Is it a hand I can touch, finger to finger on a cold and gray afternoon on any old Saturday? Is it a hand suspended in air: a hand I can begin to love the way you love the spring flowers when they bloom as if by glad instinct, a force of their own every spring, every summer, the *joyful display*— the way you held your hand up between us and I touched it by instinct, a barely discernible touch that for a small moment echoes through the empty rooms of memory? When I walk in the cold rain it is better to sing than to be silent. I know that love sings *but does not tell all its secrets.*

whenever love makes itself known

The yet unspoken may have been uttered long ago and we may have heard it already and not yet understood or we may never hear it no matter how often those words are spoken, called out, loud and clear *as if at a dissection*. As if in a book, and *a book is as perfect as a wild flower*. The rope that keeps the boat tethered to the dock; the bench that holds homeless men stretched out asleep *as if in the waiting room of a way station*; the force in our hearts that keeps love alive against *the ravages of oblivion*—glue: the gravity that keeps the stone solid on the ground and the water that holds steady inside the lake and the moon in its orbit encircling us all: glue. What is the glue that holds the sun in the sky precisely at the right distance, the right nearness, that keeps it from *descending with its gunpowder and petroleum to destroy the city*? What is the glue that keeps things from floating away, that keeps us meeting like strangers every time, held to each other with staring eyes, in the vicinity of bridges, in the gloomy awareness that *along with great cities have evolved the means to raze them to the ground*? A book of extinction that starts with *how the stars got poured into the sky*.

11

warnings from far away

A white swan with outspread wings settles among the others on a dark lake in a tactic of silence. There it swims in its own beauty amid the shadows of dark grasses reflected in the mirror smooth surface of time and *what appears most clearly is the menace*. When it glides along there are soft ripples disturbing the morning haze in its quiet—a white presence that comes as a warning I can't discern but I know it's there, just as I know the haze will lift with the warm sun as day progresses and I continue the pathway I was on. I keep going with that image in mind, the white swan I can never quite forget in its attempt *to escape its own boredom*. There was a warning there, something was wrong, they were lining up like corporals, there was a silver-like fragrance in the air and *they all seemed to suffer from homesickness*. But I keep going. One day I think this will come clear. They did not seem to know *what they were waiting for*. This will become clear to me, as transparent as the water in this dark pond with the white swans in their serenity, speaking in some unknown language the sounds of foreboding, the music of the stars, and then a sudden breeze turns everything into *sacred pollen dusting the air*.

> *He would be a poet who could impress the winds and streams into his service, to speak for him; who nailed words to their primitive senses, as farmers drive down stakes in the spring, which the frost has heaved.*
> —Henry David Thoreau

12

the day I fell in love

There is something in a strain of music which reminds me of the cries emit-ted by wild beasts in their native forests, he said. I go out among the blackberries not yet ripe and the yellow leaves of aspens in the white-trunked woods not yet matured for summer, still glowing with that lush lime-green light of expectation, down the untrodden path among the trees. There is a drive to go down that road along this *incurable imperfection*, among fences and gates with the city in the distance and the morning haze and I have no idea where I am going like some dreaming lover, the way vacationers sometimes wonder: why are we here? What did we come all this way for? The empty clay pots left on the deck are filled with sorrow, storing time *the way batteries store energy*, the rainfall of my own spiralling quest: the day I recognize *a bundle of instincts* society tried to repress, makes me want my life back, the way it was before this rush of living and feeling and before all those illusions swallowed the early light and turned everything into the blaze of day: the harsh light of breaking day, the site of *lingering catas-trophes*, and all I could have been in this world I become in another, and there is a strain of music in my mind.

13

the earth has disappeared

Day after day the rain comes down from the sky in an eternal return—
this vast, savage hovering mother of ours, Nature. The streets and drive-
ways are waterlogged. Everywhere I go the deep puddles are soaked
up by my shoes and I arrive where I'm going drenched. I see in the
falling water from above the reflections found there, mirrored in each
droplet, a view of the world, an impression of repetition and eternity,
an intuition that bears no resemblance to anything ever seen before, in
the *mutually contradictory tendencies of desire*. I walk along the boule-
vard in the pouring rain that glows *like a universe sifting its suns* in an
eternal hourglass, waiting in a sort of vertigo for the appearance of
that pink moon they promised would be out all day in the sky, confined
in the impending darkness that refuses to fire freely in its muffle of
black cloud. At such times I feel again the impulses of *a civilization
destined to have a speedy limit* and the sky is nothing but signposts as it
ties gold bundles to the feet of the moon.

14

hours of darkness

Not even does the moon shine every night, but gives place to darkness.
—Henry David Thoreau

At times I think darkness can be a wall. There is a pattern there, a face, an inscription even, but it is dirty and sad. There is writing on the wall of darkness. I am told *the hours of darkness are as necessary as the sun.* Such a strange idea, almost impossible to comprehend. But I can still think of an ordinary wall with texts and pictures, even patterns, murals, temple-like, as if those artists were imitating something else, something they heard of in a secret whisper that came to them in a dream. Many of the murals, I photograph them at times, full of life and refusal, greenhouses of anger and hurt and exhibitionism. But the archetypal wall would be a wall of Nothingness, like a Baroque church with a secret, a secret impulse to get us to an awareness, a secret thought that actually no one can read but it has meaning, *an upward-tending ecstasy.* There are letters for the child to learn, he tells me. There are drawings that tell the truth, of dark cellars with high windows where light comes in, furtively, and inside the petals of redbud blossoms they are weaving carpets of light.

15

traveler of windy expanses

All the trees of the forest fell down in the same direction after the windstorm that swept the northern hills in Sweden like an army of vengeful trolls with axes of mud in *the greatest horror fantasy every written*. We drove through there on a Sunday in August and I understood *there are more things in heaven and earth than are dreamed of in our philosophy*. Fallen tree trunks lay pointing east for miles, pale grey, thin and wispy trees that have stood their ground for decades came down in one go. It's a sight that sticks in my mind whenever I look at a stand of birches playing in the breeze like a prospectus for *enterprises not yet off the ground*, unmindful that one Sunday morning it might all be gone in a conflagration of its own. We play in the sun and then one day we're gone with the wind—first the trees, then the birds fly in with a panic looking for their tender nests in the brown rubble, then the predators, all in a big *collected work*. With its wooden brains, the forest has to remake itself, stronger next time, with deeper roots. So I learn from past disasters that spread before me like a *magic encyclopedia*: you get better, that's the hope of things, those are the *theological niceties* of how we think. Even in the daily life I lead, walking up the incline above the shoreline with the sun beaming finally after days of rain, and the unexpected happens all by itself and I find myself at the end of the line. Or I think I do. Live free, he said, *child of the mist*; forgive this dream first, then go heal the wounds of your love.

16

the loneliness of the conscious thinker

Memory can be like the tips of the fir trees shrouded in fog, or like the tops of all the trees in the forest where blossoms flower and no one sees them. In my distant memory, sculptures of Rodin were packed together in a crowded space and you could almost feel the sinewy limbs and expressive faces in their struggle to awake from the frozen dream they were in. I have forgotten the details of how the sculptures looked to me then, but I remember the feeling: how I felt, and I remember being moved by one sculpture, some quality it had of severe loneliness, of being *homesick while still at home*. And I thought of the vague sense one gets of ground and height: how heavy those works seemed in their earthiness and how light my memory of them turns out to be. How the spirit of them floats like a dense fog into the atmosphere, higher and higher until you can't see the tips of those tall trees standing in the half-light of dawn before sunrise, hardly whispering their distant aloneness to the expansive sky still lit up by electric lights of the city. Whispering in small, high tones how alone I am in the farthest reaches—the farthest reaches of what can be created and thought: the conscious loneliness of it all. The distances so great, the sound of *a golden wing barely touching the ground* as it sweeps by cannot even be heard.

17

the agony of eros

Small moments glowed with the display of illuminated particles of dust I saw from the window facing south all Saturday afternoon: with the sound of your voice and the memory of the last, mysterious star in the night that *left its impression in the sky when it went out*. There is always a remnant of stars in the firmament when I open the blinds while night is still there. I make what I call night coffee and let the blackness of space surround me, and all the small points of light. I don't want the last star in the night sky to disappear—all it needs is a passing cloud and it's gone in *an unsolved mystery*. I can see the fog float in like a kind of death in life: the obliteration of dreams and long-ing—the feeling that I need to reach something in the distance. A kind of love I feel: a kind of eros and agony for what is impossible. To long for the mystery behind the stars is a kind of love, like piercing black eyes *gleaming with vividness*. I thought about this often in the last few days: *think of suffering as being washed*, he said. There is no goal with this timeless walking except to reach through the dust of small moments and touch something that feels far away, that feels as if it could become *stone and flesh*, isolated in time, something so surprising it would seem as if *a star dropped down*.

18

the miracles that don't show up

Walking in the sunset that had a sudden glow to it made him remember
this was not the only time a light like that would form, *but it would hap-
pen forever and ever, an infinite number of evenings.* When I have looked
at you, such a light could be there and all I can think is the many years,
decades, we did not know each other and how those aeons of time
without borders are a gulf that cannot be bridged, like *dream interpreta-
tion.* The sheer distance involved, the huge chasm below that gapes
like the Grand Canyon where I hear people fall in all the time. Wayfar-
ers and tourists take one step too far in their efforts to picture them-
selves on the precipice of danger with the courage of foolhardiness.
But all I can think of is how unfamiliar the world has become, how
strange and foreign my own life seems, with the *dusty, cluttered corri-
dors* of our lives, the *kaleidoscopic distractions* and displays of ephemera
along the thresholds of doorways, knowing if we had crossed paths
long ago we may have walked past each other without a single blink of
recognition. There would have been no mutual understanding, no fall
into unknowing, and I would never have learned to *lean my starving
body against the sun.*

19

I feel the rose keep opening

He says *we saunter toward the Holy Land* when we walk. Then one day the sun will be brighter than it has ever been before. But in this house, in the end, I stand by a white radiator where the sun sends its rays at noon from the window gently onto the surface of warm pipes and a brown floor. I stand still now, with no special feelings except a lingering ambiguity that seems woven into the cashmere fabric and soft silk threads around me. We both know the power of Tibet, the proud innocence, the victories of lovers. The magical talisman, the spirit that subjugates the heart. A gold sculpture from antiquity with raised hands stands facing me and out of the sides of a red lacquer bowl prayer beads tumble out, gleaming in soft sunlight, with two brass bowls, one on each side, there for balance. I wonder why there is no tranquility after all, why it all seems just a *useless burden*, a hope and a prayer in the early afternoon. I keep thinking about the words we have read together in the early dawn: how *it will take longer to erase the self from memory than it takes for bones to disappear in their graves*. And just as with a sudden sandstorm bursting up on a dry path, *I will learn to forgive this dream*.

MOON ON FIRE

Poems/Counterpoems

In Dante Alighieri's epic poem *Paradiso*, the third book in his three-part *Divine Comedy*, the first and lowest sphere is the Sphere of the Moon. When Dante travels into the Paradisaical realms he is guided by Beatrice and introduced to the true meaning of life. He begins to understand some of his longest held questions about justice, freedom of the will, responsibility and love. Some of what he learns is counter-intuitive, but in the process he begins to separate from his old self and acquires a longing to learn to be his *true* self. In the first five Cantos, Dante asks questions about the moon, such as where its dark spots come from and how it acquires its light. He learns that everything, including the light of the moon, comes from the Sun—which is beyond his reach and which he cannot look at directly.

This impulse carries fire to the moon;
This is the motive force in mortal creatures;
This binds the earth together, makes it one.

—Dante Alighieri, *The Divine Comedy, Paradiso*, Canto 1

The lanterns of the world send a dim glow from distant places.

                    In the courtyard stands a lone plum tree,
                                        fingers of green curl
                    into a white sky, branches sway,
                    dance with the hours that pass

                like pilgrims who seek their home again.

                    This house made of blue bricks lies
        down solid against the mountain, and beyond,

                    the pale blue of distant water gleams in morning mist.

It was your light that raised me,

Dante said when he arrived at the sphere of the moon—
not alone. He was not alone.

I am thinking of the refuge of this house
with walls of wood, painted the colour of eggplant.

I walk towards the door over slices of stone

and bricks where weeds grow in the cracks.

I wanted this openness, this misty air
to breathe when the world does what it has done today:

left me without words to tell what happened.
Something happened. Something must have.

Something sailed in *across the great sea of being*—
the whole of the night sky—

I wanted to be where everything has a voice:
a wooden table with deep cracks going through;
steel benches and wicker chairs and wood stools.

To be where silence hovers,
where solitude finds rest
among stark white walls, where concrete
floors show signs of wear,

and the moon has become an *everlasting pearl*.

Blue Moon 1

They learned so fast everything they needed to know
about liberation: not to give one's life, not in war,
not in combat: but in daily life.

The routines of daily life: to change them,
customs, thoughts, prejudices—

there are many ways to die: there are many ways
to be alive, to be
free: I think these things in such a confusing space

of upholstered sofas, Steinway pianos, velvet
loungers in the centre of the room, deep
scarlet, olive green, yellow. Lamps are lit

in the middle of a sunny day. I think this sadness
really might be anger. Could it be that simple?

They were throwing colonialism into the sea
like so many rocks. It was a constant activity.

When they say there is a great wall, it is a wall
of silence.

I have not slept since you became my friend.

This is where I write my mysteries, here
on a mahogany desk, on a 1940's typewriter
under a painting of a camel and musicians

performing with curtain drawn up.

I write in a language that is not mine

but I depend on it to be myself,
a language I never chose but a language
        that has made words for my desire.

A suitcase language, I carry it with me
nomadically, furtively,
packed with the image of the self as a slave.

Packed with self-mortification, self-
consciousness, all manner of selves

performing to a row of empty seats in all the colours of the flag.

The day is well advanced. Night
arrives early now. Night with a moon
that casts a dim glow.

This is where I sleep, here
under a dark ceiling, in between the trees,

light comes in from all sides to bathe me
in the glow of a slowly journeying moon—

nomadic moon, always moving.

Environment and *nature* are not the same,
they differ
like a tidal pool and a town differ
or an owl and railroad tracks.

Last time I saw an owl it was perched completely still on a wire
looking at the window. I looked back. We stared.
It was afternoon, there was no sun.

My late father loved owls. I was thinking it was him.
It was only the last time my late father visited me
perched on a wire like a still moon, unmoving.

There is talk of *an innate bond*
they call "deep ecology." A bond
between nature and human beings.
The *natural* and the *human*.

What we love and what we surrender to.

An impulse to love and surrender,

the impulse that carries fire to the moon.

Not many are invited here, this private space
means less to others, means nothing perhaps,

sticks of incense in an old coffee tin,
rusted and disintegrated, label half-worn off,
red Folgers I think. Too much dust
collects on the neglected shelf—

large clay flower pots are full of sand where burning incense
sticks stand up like gravestones, the dead

buried along here in all their smoke. Maybe
it's a sad place, or a place full of hope. Or

a place of love. I know that now. I have known
it was love for some time now. *An eternity.*

I am surprised by love, the way it peels

the surface off in layers, the way it exposes
clay-coloured chiaroscuro shadows of doubt

and entices them into the open air, frayed
as they are, phantoms that never saw light.

        The way love reaches, *like a living flame*
        upwards, always,

the way it dissolves me *as a moth is dissolved in a flame—*

if I breathe on this delicate framework,
the dust of all my years wells up.

Never mind that old brass vessel outside,
I never knew what it was used for long ago
when new and shiny. I have not polished
anything for so long now, not since ancient

times it seems, objects have grown ugly
in my time. Or beautiful. *Very beautiful.*

Silver bells in the night sky ring

as if to invite me to a wedding, or else
to a funeral, a string of round bells

suspended over the long arc of the firmament.

I have heard the sounds of the stars,
so strange, I hardly believed it was real.

Is that sound something only I can hear,
or others like me, those who are struck

by fire, who are blinded by the glow
of the moon in the pre-dawn hours, those

of us who exist with unanswered questions
and stones in our hearts?

Black stones: I know

reason has short wings.

A dark Buddha waits in an alcove
for the perfect time to come to life, to ex-

tend a hand across the millennia, to ex-
hale the rust-red air and the silver sun,

to breathe an end to dreams, when they falter
and fall to the ground, and red banners

proclaim in a black cloud of calligraphy
as they always do:

                    you can stop now, you can

stamp that seal,
with the red wax of the heart.

Blue Moon 2

No it is not bread, not even life
we struggle for: what is freedom
if not simple dignity?

Human dignity comes at a cost when lost.

For some, life is another version of death.
Permanent resistance.

The desire for liberation,
to make your own decisions,
is the same as earth and air: *Essential,*
and it cannot be destroyed.

Not by weapons, not by lies.

The future can only come from inside;
the future does not come from a dead past.

The creation of me as you
happens in language, when you talk
across the table set with red roses
and mauve candles and a carafe of burgundy wine.

Light filters indirectly into the kitchen
trimmed in stainless steel and a photograph of scarlet lips
        intimidates the wall.

I wondered why I turned around.
Why did I turn when my name was not even called?
Why did I think that voice was addressed to me?

How we make of ourselves the subject

of subjection. What do I recognize when I hear
that voice?

I hear that is the way power works socially.
The voice of sanction,
a power that goes around on its own
without signature,

and you become attached, you fall
in love.

You are not yourself.
You are theirs.

You are caught up in *ecomimesis*—
when you speak, when you listen, when you look:

art can be a pretentious thing. Art pretends
to portray nature, evoke things in the world

107

as opposed to being what it is and always was:
a rhetorical artifact, a political function.

These words:

they do not portray you or me or even the blue moon any more.

Skyscrapers, square buildings high and low,
pierce the charcoal night with fraudulent lights

as if holding up the human world against
gravity and fate, against dark forces that press

us down, that keep us from flight, from
yearning, from awakening. I like the desire

the shining lamps represent, the longing for more

the way light reflects from a sphere in the night
and shines out, *a living pupil*—
Rows of windows brighten up after long
working hour days, walls of mirrors reflect

back to me what we had, what we lost
when we failed to act on our longings. We

locked ourselves in dark rooms of thought, we never
stepped outside into the starless night,

                                        not once—
        as if halted *by unfulfilled vows.*

    Everything is perishing *except his face,*

            yesterday's nonexistence, today's lostness, tomorrow's
                nothingness.

    I see the water at the feet of the city
    reflecting red, blue, orange from neon

    signs along the quay for Hitachi, Siemens,
    Canon, Philips, Prudential: human activity

    that won't stop. Boats and ships moored
    at the pier are strung with yellow bulbs that glow

    softly, all in a row, delicate and warm—

    So much like the extremes of love.

    Can that Art Deco tower injecting the sky
    with the substance of human endurance—

    can that structure be enough to keep us
    away from our failure, away from the grip

of a melancholy we forever invite in
to live with us?

I am told it is necessary to live in love,

it is necessary *to appease your will with love*

and *loosen the veil that covers the heart—*

I became water and was a mere mirage,
I became an ocean and was a fluff of foam,
I became aware and forgot everything,
I woke up and found myself asleep.

Blue Moon 3

What forms of identity can a *blue planet*
generate, as seen from space?

It is clear to me that to them war
is not a necessity, not an aberration, not
something that regrettably has to be done:

war for them is an
infatuation.

I cannot put it in more lucid language.

Your old country is dead. Accept it. Your new
country is not yet born.

Now everyone is a new being. You change
yourself as you change your world.

I hear you need to clear the space until it shines,
until the light flows in freely.

You talk about your nation, but why not talk
about *borderlands, nomadism, border-
crossings*? Things unsettled.

The blue planet is never stable.
Never was.

Dissolution and destruction
do not come from elsewhere.

It is I who act but the act is not mine,
it is I who speak but the words are not mine,
it is I who desire, but the desire is not mine
either.

I hear in order to persist *you need to want to die.*

       While the courtyard cherry trees are in bloom
       and while the Chinese lanterns glow with small light

       from hooks on the heavy wall, and while
       the bed curtains are drawn open and the tea is warm
       on the tea tray, all morning long:

you think you live normally, things look normal,

but inside you want to disappear,

to vanish *like a heavy thing that sinks in deep water.*

       who is the one who hears in my ears?
       who is the one who speaks words in my mouth?
       who is the one who sees through my eyes?
       who is the one who wears me?

112

A bright yellow bicycle is parked against
the rampart; a high Banyan tree stands in the pale

white air; Italian silk cushions lie
on the deck and scarlet curtains fold at the window—
all placed there *as if life were theatre.*

Life is not theatre, though it's treated
that way. Performances day after day.

Silk screens and gold embroidered cloth
and tassels tie drapes into folds,
Art Deco railings line the stairs—

a solid performance. I admit I enjoy the show,

the escape, flight, forgetting, prevailing
 against the possibilities I won't face.

I don't know what is so fearful—
is it the thought of you that won't leave me,

the image of you—not your face, not your eyes,
 but the you behind you, behind your eyes,

the way you are able to gaze directly
 into mine, without pressure or impulse,

your gaze, how it arrives out of deep space-
how I am left suspended, strangely alive
the way a lamp glows at midnight,
                              softly.

I have paced this old Tibetan rug so often
I begin to see the pattern my feet have made
in the ancient silk. I have watched the canvas

on the dark red wall, depicting a woman
in black, seated under the lamplight her-
self. I have traced the lines on the floor,

red and white, drawn them over and over.

What I wonder is how the violence of others
diminishes me?

It was a question Dante once asked in his confusion too—

why should the violence of others cause
the measure of my merit to be less?

Blue Moon 4

Colonialism itself is a sower of seeds:

seeds of doubt, half-truths, outright lies,
self-recrimination, violence, suicide.

You have become your own colonizer.

You are now the victim and the perpetrator;
you have reduced yourself to silence

in someone else's name.

Your own thought:
they took it from you,
they made it their own.

It can take a whole lifetime to learn
how to live your own life.

How to tell your own story.

Storyteller.

Paradise in the Sea of Sorrow.

You have become a colonized subject like so many bonsai trees
in pots along the veranda,
or so many silk lanterns above the pagoda.

There are votives in glass cups bunched on the table
where stone Buddhas crouch quietly.

They have not only changed you, they have
created you.
    Before them, there was no you,

there was a torso without legs, a broken body
with one arm,

    there was snow in the field
and the air was still with cold.
When someone dies, Dante says

their soul returns to that same star
from which it had been taken—

    The jagged cliffs and overhanging tree
    trunks and branches, the soft, pale green

    haze-touched forest leaves, all glitter
    in a silver-tinged morning.

    I feel I have flown here on unearthly wings, somehow
    I managed to pass over the old stone ruins

    on the tips of grey mountains. The soil
     is dry. The distance is blurred by low cloud.

If we could only be here alone and leave
the past behind, the way dawn
leaves the night behind, or dusk parts

with the preceding day where too much
went on, too many people pressed and pushed.

Now that I dream the dreams of longing
for quiet, silence, to be alone with you.

A swan settles on the dark pond
reflecting green trees and stone walls
of timeless country houses with clay
roofs and wooden railings and hanging
baskets of peonies suspended in air.

A quiet presence that comes as
a warning I can't discern
but I know it's there just as I know

the haze will lift with the warm
sun as day progresses—

I follow a trail that goes up the cliff-
side and a road that leads out of the gate,

for there is a quiet presence looming wherever I look.

For they have given feet and hands to God
but they mean something else.

They mean everything that is not him
is leading you to walk the wrong path.

Blue Moon 5

Your life has been *destructured*.

In its place there is a pile of unwanted things:
judgments, stories, reasons, laws that confine you

in a chamber of guilt. All the time. Everywhere.

You now need permission to be yourself,
from whom, you're never sure.

Even to change yourself, or to assimilate
into what, you're never sure.

You now need permission to resist
what you are resisting.

It becomes necessary to oppose yourself,
your colonized self, first. Your own fear,
your own despair.

You have your secrets. You have
a veil of secrecy,
a white curtain that trails onto the floor
and barely hides what lies behind.

The city stretches its fingers, the long canals sleep,
stone bridges arrive at intervals, and benches
are parked where I can rest and look at the water.

A gramophone, His Master's Voice, is placed
squarely in the middle of everything
its speaker jutting into the room like a tornado.

My world persists only in repetitions.

My world persists only by turning
against myself: my conscience, my
melancholia, my bereavement—

turning in place,

round and round like a vinyl record.

The columns are bright red. The walls are stark white.

The gramophone records are piled in disarray.

He and I became acquainted,
and it was he who made me acquainted with him through him.

I am bewildered *in the highest degree, in what was*

before everything and what will be after
the passing away of everything.

Rumi says, reach for the cup of the Beloved

and *drink the wine.*

In the earliest hours I barely discern
the rooftops of low buildings. Small windows
and balconies line the facades, white and brown.

The smell of coffee ascends in the bare kitchen,
spices stand lined up in the corner, an old bird

cage waits without a bird, a dining table once used
for billiards stands solid, and a face so smooth and somber

hovers above, eyes half closed, lips red

the colour of red roses in a vase.

I can see the rain has fallen overnight.
Planks on the balcony glisten wet,

                              the stone statue,
Buddha with hand up, is weeping.

An empty teapot still stands on the red
lacquer table, with two empty cups.

A bamboo screen shields us from the light
when morning appears, slowly inch by inch.

I left them there to remember you by.
Our moment that came and went, a moment

all ours. I regretted its passing even before
it passed: I saw a future without this one

moment we had, we stole from somewhere,
we, thieves.

This regret, this immediate sense of loss,
is it a kind of love?

Everything is silent now. The yellow
curtains drape themselves across the window
in folds and curves. The small table lamp

cradles an even smaller light in paper hands
the way I cradle what I begin to think is

a kind of love.

Dante says in Paradise, *to mortal eyes*
there justice seems unjust—

It was Jerjis who was killed seventy times.

He came back to life *seventy times*.

Blue Moon 6

You learn to expel yourself.

You learn to expel yourself from your own body.

You learn your own disfigurement.

You become a fatalist. You no longer react
to the faces of adversity.

*To flee menace
you end up doing what should not be done.*

Their voices are harsh, cutting, metallic,
accusatory. Their voices are violent—
the sound is directly directed at you.

Your sense that life is a permanent struggle
against death is you,

colonized. You live the life of in-
complete death.

You are assumed dead. Even now
as you breathe the same air as I.

You thought you would find rest. *You found only
a bad conscience.*

The voice I hear is dominant
and indifferent. I notice the contrast,

how it is directed at me and also at no one.

A disembodied voice without signature.

I cannot answer back to such a voice.
It is not a conversation.

I confusedly sit on this wooden stool and look at my books.

I have left the front door open for fresh air,
but it is the air of the city, of smog

                                        and exhaust.

This is the city of existence—

              rose and mirror and sun and moon—where are they?

              In my bamboo house that crouches
              like a turtle on the side of the mountain

where hard cliffs protrude, scattered
with brush and small snow and light

air, so light you can hardly breathe,
my escape from a cold, wet city—

in my bamboo house the sun is yellow
and the shadows line up in rows when

a pale sun shines through the glass.

My bamboo house is my hermitage,
my refuge, even from you now, from the dark

that has formed around you, the aspect
of night that covers you like a veil,

what they call reality. Such times I think
of the lone bamboo in its earthen jar

at the end of the hallway, and the mirror-
shiny floors reflecting daylight and wood,

soft hills outside the big window
streaked with outcroppings of rock,

where birds on light wings occasionally pass—
my bamboo house teaches me

to learn to love daily life, suspended breath,
filigree memories just as they are,

solitude or company, desert hills

and naked rooms that echo among the walls:

beloved of the first lover,

there is a truth beyond whose boundaries no truth lies.

Blue Moon 7

You cannot bring your life to a standstill, you cannot
stop long enough to look back.

Time never gives you perfect repose.

You think you need that stasis now
to hold off the catastrophe of progress.

You fetishize all the concepts of the world.

You think you can ward off
the enemies at the gate, but you cannot.

You are the enemy yourself.

There is only moving forward now,
there is only you and the sun and the moon now,

and the sun is ablaze and the moon is on fire.

You want to see evidence of your own existence.

Anything outside of you: objects, words, signs.

In your barren space you shield your eyes from the sun
with wooden screens. You lie down on your straw rug
and you drink water that never gets cold.

You would give a lot to be visible.
You look at yourself with others' eyes.

It is not possible to see yourself as yourself.

Your grief is incomplete. You berate yourself
with melancholy.

You wanted to grieve the loss of a love
you were never able to love, a love that never
was found and yet was lost.

To grieve that you refused to love.

You wanted to destroy
a love that would destroy you.

You always knew it is not your world
but it is the world in which you live.

A world of chalk and wooden stairs and light bulbs.

You knew there was a never-ending light that
once seen, alone and always, kindles love.

There is only you and the sun and the moon now

and the sun is ablaze and the moon is on fire.

The sun is still high in the sky. As it ever was,
the sun has the face of everything.

I try not to tell only stories of decline,

how everything is degraded and ruined.

You, me, everything. That *declensions narrative*,

that is not the only story.

Are you far or are you near?
Should I call or should I whisper?

When I love him, I am his hearing through which he hears, his eyesight through which he sees, his hand through which he holds, and his foot through which he walks.

—Hadīth Qudsī

Credits

"A Moment in Flight" was first published in essay form as a chapbook by Above/Ground Press, Ottawa, in 2020.

www.ingramcontent.com/pod-product-compliance
Lightning Source LLC
Chambersburg PA
CBHW022011090426
42741CB00007B/983